Compass Point
Phonics Readers

What Is in the Sky?

by Cindy Chapman

Reading Consultant: Wiley Blevins, M.A.
Phonics/Early Reading Specialist

Compass Point Books
3109 West 50th Street, #115
Minneapolis, MN 55410

Visit Compass Point Books on the Internet at *www.compasspointbooks.com*
or e-mail your request to *custserv@compasspointbooks.com*

Photographs ©: Cover and p. 1: Index Stock Imagery/Alan Bolesta, p. 6: Index Stock
Imagery/Wallace Garrison, p. 7: PhotoDisc/Hisham F. Ibrahim, p. 8: Photo Researchers,
Inc./John Sanford, p. 9: DigitalVision, p. 10: Index Stock Imagery/David Carriere, p. 11:
DigitalVision, p. 12: Corbis/Mug Shots

Editorial Development: Alice Dickstein, Alice Boynton
Photo Researcher: Wanda Winch
Design/Page Production: Silver Editions, Inc.

Library of Congress Cataloging-in-Publication Data
Chapman, Cindy.
  What is in the sky? / by Cindy Chapman.
     p. cm. — (Compass Point phonics readers)
  Includes index.
  Summary: Introduces what can be seen in the daytime and nighttime
  sky—especially the sun, moon, and stars--in an easy-to-read text that
  incorporates phonics instruction.
   ISBN 0-7565-0513-5 (hardcover : alk. paper)
   1. Astronomy—Juvenile literature. 2. Reading—Phonetic
  method—Juvenile literature. [1. Astronomy. 2. Sky. 3. Reading—
  Phonetic method.] I. Title. II. Series.
   QB46.C483 2004
   520—dc21   2003006357

Table of Contents

Dear Parent or Caregiver,

Welcome to Compass Point Phonics Readers, books of information for young children. Each book concentrates on specific phonic sounds and words commonly found in beginning reading materials. Featuring eye-catching photographs, every book explores a single science or social studies concept that is sure to grab a child's interest.

So snuggle up with your child, and let's begin. Start by reading aloud the Mother Goose nursery rhyme on the next page. As you read, stress the words in dark type. These are the words that contain the phonic sounds featured in this book. After several readings, pause before the rhyming words, and let your child chime in.

Now let's read *What Is in the Sky?* If your child is a beginning reader, have him or her first read it silently. Then ask your child to read it aloud. For children who are not yet reading, read the book aloud as you run your finger under the words. Ask your child to imitate, or "echo," what he or she has just heard.

Discussing the book's content with your child:
Explain to your child that the moon seems to shine, but it does not give off its own light. It is really reflecting light from the sun.

At the back of the book is a fun Batter Up! game. Your child will take pride in demonstrating his or her mastery of the phonic sounds and the high-frequency words.

Enjoy Compass Point Phonics Readers and watch your child read and learn!

A Crooked Man

There was a **crooked** man,
And he walked a **crooked** mile.
He found a **crooked** sixpence
Against a **crooked** stile;
He bought a **crooked** cat,
Which caught a **crooked** mouse,
And they all lived together
In a little **crooked** house.

In the daytime, you can see many things in the sky. You can see clouds. You can see the sun. You can see birds.

In the nighttime, you see different things. On many nights you can see the moon. The moon is the brightest light in the sky at night.

Sometimes the moon is full. It looks round like a circle. Sometimes it looks curved like part of a circle. Sometimes you can't see the moon at all.

On a clear night you can see
many stars, too. They give off light.
Stars are much bigger than Earth.
They look small because they are
very far away.

Did you know the sun is a star?
The sun's light makes the sky bright
in the daytime. The sun's heat
warms Earth.

The sun is the star closest to Earth. The sun is still very far away. It is much bigger than Earth, but it looks smaller because it is so far away.

Go outside at night. Look up at the sky. What do you see?

Word List

Variant Vowels

/o͞o/
do

moon

to

too

/o͝o/
look(s)

full

High-Frequency
because

off

Science
circle

different

Earth

warms

Batter Up!

You will need:
- 1 penny
- 2 moving pieces, such as nickels or checkers

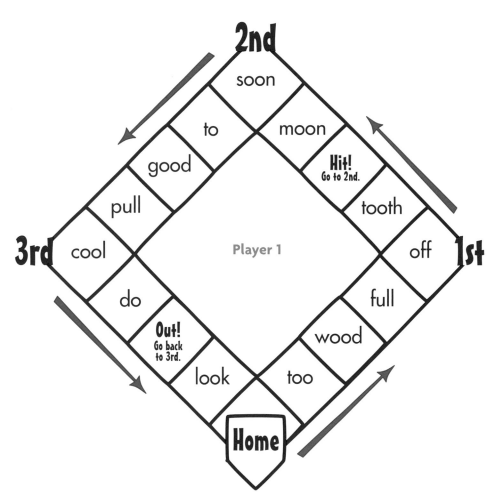

2nd

soon

to   moon

good   **Hit!** Go to 2nd.

pull   tooth

3rd cool   **Player 1**   off **1st**

do   full

Out! Go back to 3rd.   wood

look   too

Home

14

How to Play

- Put the moving pieces on Home. The first player shakes the penny and drops it on the table. Heads means move 1 space. Tails means move 2 spaces.
- The player moves and reads the word. If the child does not read the word correctly, tell him or her what it is. On the next turn, the child must read the word before moving.
- A run is scored by the first player to arrive at Home plate, and the inning is over. Continue playing out the number of innings previously decided. The player with the most runs wins.

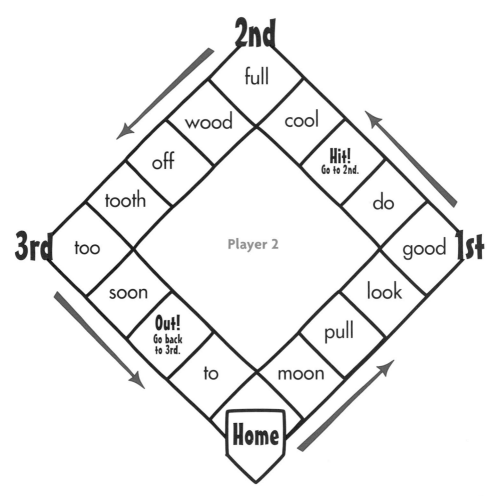

Read More

Bredeson, Carmen. *The Moon.* Rookie Read-About Science Series. New York: Children's Press, 2003.

Rau, Dana Meachen. *The Solar System.* Simply Science Series. Minneapolis, Minn.: Compass Point Books, 2001.

Rustad, Martha E.H. *The Stars.* Out in Space Series. Mankato, Minn.: Pebble Books, 2002.

Tesar, Jenny E. *The Planets.* Space Observer Series. Des Plaines, Ill.: Heinemann Interactive Library, 1998.

Index